VIEWS

ON THE

FREE NAVIGATION OF THE ST. LAWRENCE,

REPORTED

BY MR. BUEL,

ACCOMPANY JOINT RESOLUTION ON THE SAME SUBJECT FROM THE COMMITTEE ON FOREIGN AFFAIRS.

IN THE HOUSE OF REPRESENTATIVES, MAY 2, 1850

WASHINGTON:
PRINTED AT UNION OFFICE.
1850.

FREE NAVIGATION OF THE ST. LAWRENCE.

[To accompany Joint Resolution No. 19.]

May 2, 1850.

Mr. Buel, from the Committee on Foreign Affairs, made the following

REPORT:

The Committee on Foreign Affairs, to whom were referred sundry petitions of citizens of the United States residing in States adjacent to the northern chain of lakes, and the memorial of the legislature of the State of Wisconsin, praying Congress to adopt measures for securing to American commerce the right of freely navigating the St. Lawrence, and also joint resolutions of the legislature of the State of Michigan relative to the same subject, report:

That they have had the subject under consideration, and they recommend the adoption of the following resolution:

Resolved by the Senate and House of Representatives of the United States of America in Congress assembled, That the free navigation of the St. Lawrence river, for commercial purposes, demands the earnest attention of the American government; and that it is highly desirable that it be secured to American commerce at an early day.

31st Congress, 1st Session. | Rep. No. 295. | Ho. of Reps.

FREE NAVIGATION OF THE ST. LAWRENCE.

May 2, 1850.

Mr. Buel, from the Committee on Foreign Affairs, presented the following views of a portion of the committee; which were ordered to be printed:

[TO ACCOMPANY REPORT 295.]

The undersigned, members of the Committee on Foreign Affairs, to whom were referred sundry petitions of citizens of the United States residing in States adjacent to the northern chain of lakes, and the memorial of the legislature of the State of Wisconsin, praying Congress to adopt measures for securing to American commerce the right of freely navigating the St. Lawrence, and also joint resolutions of the legislature of the State of Michigan relative to the same subject, ASSENTING *to the resolution reported by the committee, also report their reasons:*

The free navigation of the St. Lawrence, from its connexion with the chain of lakes to the ocean, presents a question somewhat new in the history of the government. In its early agitation, its importance was more prospective than present; and hence, after various unsuccessful attempts to settle it by negotiation with Great Britain, it was allowed to slumber until a more urgent occasion should call for its decision.

The future, which then seemed distant, has suddenly become a present reality, and the wonderful growth of our inland commerce of the lakes has revived the question and given to it fresh interest. The government is now called upon to adopt measures for securing a commercial privilege of great local and national importance. Final action upon the subject will determine whether the export productions of the Northwest and the States adjacent to the lakes may, in part, find their way to the markets of the world through the ocean-outlet of nature, or be disadvantageously forced through the interrupted, contracted, and circuitous channels of art. It will in fact determine whether the millions who dwell and are to dwell in the valley of the lakes shall be permitted to seek intercourse with remote countries by a gentle and easy descent to the ocean, thus appropriating the St. Lawrence as a natural highway to the purposes for which it was designed by Providence, or whether they must divert streams from their native beds, fell forests, fill up valleys, bridge chasms, and even climb or penetrate mountains, in order to maintain such intercourse.

Whoever will look at this question in its length and breadth will not wonder that it now presses itself upon the attention of the country as a great practical question. The laws of nature, the wants of the people, the commercial interests of the country, and even the necessities of the case, conspire to present the question as one which must ere long be decided, either by legislation or negotiation, or by that great current of events which overrides human effort, and accomplishes ends in spite of all resistance.

Nor is the question one of mere local importance. The St. Lawrence forms part of the long chain of waters which lies upon our northern boundary, as did once the Mississippi upon our western; and the question of freely navigating the latter was not much less national in its nature than is that of freely navigating the former.

A full examination of the subject requires some notice of the fact that our government has hitherto claimed the right of freely navigating the St. Lawrence as a *natural* right. It was upon this basis that the claim was urged and supported with great power and ability. It was resisted by Great Britain, and the discussion terminated without its settlement. The claim of right is believed to stand now as it did then, save that new events have given it new strength. The subject, therefore, presents itself in a twofold aspect—

1. As a right, to be claimed by the government.
2. As a privilege, to be secured by treaty, or some reciprocal legislation.

We do not propose to discuss at great length the natural right of the United States to a free passage to the ocean through the waters of the St. Lawrence. Whilst but few arguments can be added to those which were urged nearly a generation since in its support, it is yet worthy of notice that the experience of the present day has so clearly proved their justice and validity. The wants and necessities of the extensive region of the lakes, which were then so plainly shadowed forth in the future, have now come to exist, and confirm the justice of our claim. It is therefore deemed well to revive, if not to press, this view of the subject, so that, if the government shall at last conceive itself compelled to purchase as a privilege that which justly belonged to it as a right, its action may appear, what it really will be, a measure of necessity, resulting from the unwillingness of England to acknowledge the justice of our claim. In such an event, it will be but just that the transaction should stand forth in its true character in the history of her intercourse with us; whilst, however, the unconditional acknowledgment of our right by Great Britain would be received by the people of this country with the liveliest satisfaction, and could not fail to have a powerful influence in convincing them of her disposition to treat us with justice and liberality, and in confirming the good understanding which now happily prevails between the two countries.

Although the right of the United States freely to navigate the St. Lawrence to the ocean may have existed from the definitive acknowledgment of our independence by Great Britain in 1783, and even from the treaty of Paris in 1763, which secured to her the Canadas, and of course to her, in common with her adjacent colonies, the use and control of that river throughout its whole extent, yet, as a *question*, it is modern in its origin. So long as there was no occasion for exercising the right, there was none for asserting or disputing it. It is true, under the supposition that the sources of the Mississippi were within the British boundaries as established by the treaty of 1783, that instrument contained a stipulation that "the navigation of the river Mississippi, *from its source to the ocean*, shall forever remain free and open to the subjects of Great Britain and the citizens of the United States,'' whilst it was silent upon the subject of navigating the St. Lawrence. The cases were undoubtedly analogous as regards the *natural* right of navigating similar outlets to the ocean, but in some respects they were widely different. We cannot fail to perceive that, by this stipulation, the two countries claimed the free navigation of the Mississippi from its source to the ocean on the *natural* right alone, *for that claim was thus put forth in the treaty, without any arrangement with Spain, by whom the mouth of that river was then held.* But this feature in the case deserves more particular notice in another connexion.

It must also be observed that the cases were widely different in respect to the supposed relative importance of the two rivers. The situation of the mouth of the Mississippi in reference to the Gulf of Mexico and the West Indies, the continuance of navigation for more than a thousand miles above its mouth at all seasons of the year, and its character as an extensive national boundary, well indicated the future importance of the river, and the wisdom of securing, if possible, the right of freely navigating its waters. But the future value of the St. Lawrence was then estimated by different circumstances. It was ice-bound for one-half of the year. It was contiguous to but one of the States, (New York,) and for but a small part of its northern boundary; and even here the habitation of the white man was seldom, if ever, to be found. We had no commerce, no property, afloat upon this river, unless in the bark canoe and emanating from the small trading posts among the Indians upon the upper lakes. Even this trade was carried on with Montreal, and was essentially Canadian in its character. The geography of all this region was but little understood in our own country, much less in Europe; and some of its natural curiosities were there known very much as wonderful traditions or fables. Detroit existed only as a trading post; whilst Buffalo, (which now rivals even the ancient capital of New York,) Cleveland, Chicago, and Milwaukie, were then unknown. The great valley of the lakes was without people, without commerce. Whilst they were viewed as a waste of waters, their shores were skirted for thousands of miles by one continuous wilderness.

Besides, canals were at this time unknown in our country. It was gravely published in London, about the middle of the last century, in an extensive geographical and historical work, that the Falls of Niagara are six hundred feet in height, and, at the period of the acknowledgment of our independence by Great Britain, they were doubtless regarded as an insurmountable barrier against all connexion by navigation of the upper lakes with the waters of the St. Lawrence. In fact, no human wisdom could foresee that what then seemed to be the work of centuries was destined to be accomplished in one or two generations. Still less could human wisdom foresee that these lakes would so soon teem with a commerce that should demand the use of that highway to the ocean which was provided for it by nature. Had the wonderful realities of the present been thought or dreamed of, and our natural right under such circumstances questioned, at the period of the treaty of '83, can any one doubt that we should have demanded a stipulation for the free navigation of the St. Lawrence, and that such stipulation would have been as readily arranged as that for the free navigation of the Mississippi?

We have submitted the preceding observations for the purpose of showing that the question of our right to the navigation of the St. Lawrence could not have existed as a practical question at the period of the treaty of '83, but is one of subsequent and modern origin. We have desired to show that it could not exist as a practical question until the country of the lakes came to be inhabited and civilized, and to teem with a commerce seeking its natural channel in this ocean-outlet. That period has now come, and with a rapidity far beyond the conceptions of our ancestors. The spirit of enterprise and adventure, which at an early day in our history sent the American pioneer to the foot of the Alleghanies, has carried his descendants far over and beyond this barrier, and planted their habitations on the shores of those great lakes upon whose waters they now ask to be borne in their downward passage to the ocean.

Having thus briefly noticed the origin and history of our claim, we come next to a consideration of the arguments upon which it rests.

Nature plainly points to the ocean as a field of enterprise for the whole world, and international law recognises it as property to be enjoyed in common by all nations. While nature has thus provided the world with a common highway, she has been lavish in also providing for inland nations lesser highways or means of access to it, such as inlets and rivers. The right of all nations jointly to navigate the ocean may well be deduced from the fact that it is the common reservoir formed by a union of the lesser highways or rivers, which, to a certain degree, are recognised as the property of the contiguous nations through whose territories they pass, to the extent of their contiguity. This property is justly qualified by the claim of upper and inland nations to the right of passage to and from the ocean; and this right of ingress and egress asserts but little more than the national right of using and following a national qualified property until it reaches the ocean or common reservoir, where all stand upon equal footing.

A nation may well assert control over a river flowing in its whole length through its own territories. So, too, by analogy, may a nation assert control over the sources or upper parts of a river, so far as they lie within its boundaries. Such right interferes with the interests of no nation below in seeking passage to and from its mouth, and prosecuting its trade and commerce upon the ocean. But is it not a very different case, when a nation, by discovery, settlement, or conquest, takes possession of the mouth of a great ocean-outlet, which, it may be, extends inland for thousands of miles, washes and fertilizes the soil of various climates and countries, and is the only natural highway of many nations equally sovereign with that which may chance to own the soil contiguous to its mouth? What process of reasoning, or what plea of convenience or necessity, in such case, can concentrate in the lower nation a sovereignty which overrides and absorbs all sovereignties above, or give to the lower sovereignty a greater right of navigation than that which belongs to the upper? The language of the protocol referred to in the letter of Mr. Rush, when minister to England, to Mr. Adams, the American Secretary of State, dated August 12, 1823, well confirms the preceding view:

"It has sometimes been said that the possession by one nation of both the shores of a river at its mouth gives the right of obstructing the navigation of it to the people of other nations living on the banks above; but it remains to be shown upon what satisfactory grounds the assumption by the nation below of exclusive jurisdiction over a river thus situated can be placed. The common right to navigate it is, on the other hand, a right of nature. This is a principle which, it is conceived, will be found to have the sanction of the most revered authorities of ancient and modern times; and if there have been temporary occasions when it has been questioned, it is not known that the reasons upon which it rests, as developed in the most approved works upon public law, have ever been impugned.

"There is no sentiment more deeply and universally felt than that the ocean is free to all men, and the waters that flow into it to those whose home is upon their shores. In nearly every part of the world we find this natural right acknowledged, by laying navigable rivers open to all the inhabitants of their banks; and wherever the stream, entering the limits of another society or nation, has been interdicted to the upper inhabitants, it has been an act of *force* by a stronger against a weaker party, and condemned by the judgment of mankind. The right of the upper inhabitants to the full use of the stream rests upon the same imperious want as that of the lower—upon the same intrinsic necessity of participating in the benefits of this flowing element."

Let us now inquire into the nature of this right of sovereignty over navigable rivers passing through different countries. The *natural* law clearly points to them as highways common to the nations which dwell upon their banks. The law of nations likens them to highways, and such, it is believed, they are defined to be by the statute law of nearly all civilized countries. But the control of ordinary highways is by no means absolute in the ruling sovereignty. They are appropriated by human as well as natural laws to certain specific purposes, which are inconsistent with the unqualified right of any power to dispose of them at will. The individual, subject, or citizen, the *natural man*, possesses rights here which even the sovereignty cannot justly annul or take from him without rendering compensation. The instructions of Mr. Adams to Mr. Rush in 1823 upon this subject are so pertinent to this view, that they deserve to be quoted: "The right of navigating the river is a right of nature, preceding it in point of time, and which the sovereign right of one nation cannot annihilate, as belonging to the people of another." Upon this point, Mr. Rush pressed our claim on the British government in the very terms of his instructions.

The principle relied on points to, and springs from, the natural right of every human creature to the enjoyment of life, liberty, and happiness, and to the use of all those just means which are necessary to give effect to that right. The existing sovereignty may *regulate* the use of a highway, but it has no right, in ordinary cases, to close or destroy it, without compensating individual losses. Such avenues are for the use of the public—of the individuals composing the ruling state. The right to a highway is the right to use it, to travel in it, to pass and repass. It is created, whether artificial or natural, not so much for the accommodation of nations in their sovereign capacity, as of the individuals who dwell near them, and who, without them, could not prosecute the ordinary pursuits and occupations of civilized life. Is it not evident, then, that the sovereignty which a nation is said to possess over its highways is, substantially and for practical purposes, the right of the *individual man* to use them for those objects for which they were originally designed?

Let us now apply these views more directly to the case of navigable rivers. They are held to be highways by the courts of England and of this country, and the right of using them is likened to that of using a highway. The English and American law treatises and decisions are full of authority to this effect, and it is unnecessary to cite them. It is worthy of remark that Congress, as early as 1786, affirmed this view in respect to the navigable waters leading into the Mississippi and St. Lawrence. This was done by a resolution adopted in that year; and the same view was afterwards reaffirmed in the ordinance of 1787, which, in the very language of the resolution cited, declares the said waters and the carrying places between the same "to be common highways, and forever free, as well to the inhabitants of the said territory as to the citizens of the United States and those of any other States that may be admitted into the confederacy, without any tax, impost, or duty therefor." The right of freely navigating the Mississippi to its mouth had already been asserted by the United States, and the resolution cited and the ordinance of 1787 extended that right to the navigable tributaries of both rivers.

How, then, stands the case of the St. Lawrence? It is a large navigable river, emptying directly into the ocean. For several hundred miles above its mouth, it is substantially a great ocean-inlet, averaging not less than thirty miles in width. Above, the American sovereignty rules upon one bank and the English upon the other; whilst below, both are ruled by the latter. It is a national highway; and the right to navigate it is the right to use it, to apply it to those purposes for which it was designed by the God of nature. The right of navigation in this case, as in that of a highway, is the right of the *individual*, the *natural* man; and the ruling sovereignty is absolute in neither. In fact, that sovereignty or control which a nation claims for itself over a navigable river passing within its borders is substantially the right of its people—its individual citizens or subjects—to use it according to its natural design of furnishing them with a pathway to the ocean, and enabling them to hold intercourse with the remote nations of the globe. How, then, can those who dwell upon the upper parts of a navigable stream lose the right of freely passing on it to and from the ocean by happening not to dwell under the sovereignty of that people who occupy its lower banks? How can it be shown that a mere difference of local position can thus operate to diminish or enlarge a natural right which exists and belongs to man independently of all human government?

To such views as these may be added the authority of Mr. Clay, who, when he was Secretary of State, in his instructions of June 19, 1826, to Mr. Gallatin, our minister at London, used the following language: "It is inconceivable upon what just grounds a nation below can oppose the right of that above to pass through a great natural highway into the sea, that it may trade or hold intercourse with other nations by their consent. From the very nature of such a river, it must, in respect to its navigable uses, be considered as common to all the nations who inhabit its banks, as a free gift flowing from the bounty of Heaven, intended for all whose lots are cast upon its borders." And in his instructions of the 8th of August, in the same year, to Mr. Gallatin, he says, concerning the right of navigating the St. Lawrence, independently of Great Britain: "Nor can the President consent to any treaty by which they should renounce that right, expressly or by implication."

The right to *regulate* the use of a highway—as a navigable river—must not be confounded with an absolute sovereignty. This right of *regulation* must necessarily belong to the contiguous nations; but it must be exercised consistently with the prior natural right of navigation. Laws and government should extend as well over the waters as the banks of a river, and they form what may be called the local jurisdiction. But the prior right of navigation overrides all local law, and cannot be annulled, for it existed *before* and exists *independently* of all law. The right may be regulated under law by considerations of justice and expediency, but it cannot be destroyed. The right of navigating the ocean furnishes an apt illustration of the distinction thus taken. No one will deny that it is a natural right, and exists independently of law; but its exercise brought into existence new circumstances and relations between nations, which rendered necessary some law for the regulation of such exercise. Here we see the origin of international maritime law, which asserts jurisdiction over the ocean, furnishes it with a government, and *regulates* without destroying the prior right. It is only in this sense that a nation can be said to have sovereign power over the mouth of a navigable river, as against another occupying above. This same distinction was evidently taken by Mr. Adams in his instructions to Mr. Rush, before referred to, and in the following terms: "The exclusive *right of jurisdinction* over a river originates in the social compact, and is a right of sovereignty. The *right of navigating* the river is a right of nature, preceding it in point of time, and which the sovereign right of one nation cannot annihilate, as belonging to the people of another." The Congress of Vienna, in 1815, whilst it provided for the free navigation of many of the rivers of Europe, did not omit also to provide that "the regulations established with regard to the *police* of this navigation" should be respected—thus plainly recognising a right of jurisdiction as distinct from that of navigation.

We have now reached that point in the argument upon the nature of national sovereignty over navigable rivers emptying into the ocean where we are prepared to assert it is seldom, if ever, *absolute* and *unqualified.* It does not exist in the case of a navigable stream situate entirely within the territory of a single nation; for it is subject to the prior natural right of those who have planted their homes upon its banks, and must be exercised consistently with that right. It does not exist in the case of a nation dwelling upon any part above its mouth, or, it may be, occupying exclusively its sources; for, in that case, such nation, exercising its absolute sovereignty, could divert the stream, and thus destroy the navigation of nations occupying below. Lastly, it does not exist in the case of a nation holding the mouth; for if, as we have just seen, a nation occupying above cannot possess it, by what principle of justice can it be shown that a nation occupying below can possess it, thus establishing, in respect to sovereignty over a navigable river, an unequal rule of right amongst those who have chosen to settle upon its borders, and who, though from necessity they must occupy different positions in regard to its mouth, and dwell at different distances from the sea, yet all settled upon its borders for the same purpose of using it, of navigating it, of trading with remote nations, of passing and repassing at will between their homes and the ocean?

Further, if Great Britain contends for an absolute national sovereignty over the mouths of navigable rivers which may be in her possession, is she prepared to submit to the consequences which naturally flow from it, and seem quite as reasonable as the doctrine itself? The doctrine, it is true, does not go quite so far as to imply absolute property in the contiguous water, as in land or moveable articles; for the water by necessity would cease to become such when it passes from one territorial dominion into another. It is continuous in its nature; and the same water forms the navigable river both above and below the dividing boundary line. Yesterday it was in one dominion, to-day it is in another, and "to-morrow will be in that ocean to which the presumptuous sway of no one has as yet been lawfully extended." Whilst the doctrine does not go to the length just intimated, it does, however, give as absolute and sovereign control over the *sources* of a river to a nation within whose territories they are situate, as over the *mouth* to that nation which may possess it. Such control is as just and consistent with the principles of right in one case as in the other.

Apply this consequence of the doctrine claimed to the case of the St. Lawrence, and what follows? Its chief sources are the great lakes, one of which lies *entirely* within American territory. It has been believed that the waters of Lake Erie can be made to flow into the Ohio. This idea is not altogether new; for such a connexion, in the form of a canal, was the subject of correspondence between Washington and Jefferson at an early day in the history of the country. It was then supposed that it might be the means of bringing the trade of the western country to Virginia. Whatever might be the effects of such a measure at the present day, by way of diverting trade, if feasible, it might be so executed as to create a new and large navigable river within our borders, which, whilst it would form a great highway for inland commerce, would at the same time swell the waters of the Ohio so as to be navigable by steamboats at all seasons of the year for a much greater distance above its mouth. But would England acquiesce in such a measure, when she should suddenly find the waters of the St. Lawrence partially dried up, and its navigation from Lake Ontario to Quebec perhaps destroyed by *shoals, rocks,* and *rapids?*

Yet this case, extreme as it may seem, would be the natural result of the doctrine for which England contends. It could work but little injury to us, except so far as the St. Lawrence may be contiguous to New York. Lake Ontario is of great depth, and, although its outlet would become greatly diminished, yet its surface would be but little affected, and its navigation would continue as before. The upper lakes would remain the same, as their surplus waters would still accumulate in, and be discharged from, Lake Erie. But this objection would be without force, since our drainage of its surplus waters would not injure its navigation.

Yielding, however, to this objection, let us pass upward for a thousand miles, and we come to the extremity of Lake Michigan, which lies *entirely* within our borders. It cannot be denied that the United States have as sovereign control over the waters of this lake as any nation can have over those of a navigable river. But will England admit such control to be absolute and unqualified, and allow us to drain its waters into the Ohio or Mississippi? In this case, as in the other, she might behold her navigation of the St. Lawrence obstructed by new shoals, rocks, and rapids. Michigan, too, might be a little interested in this state of things; and all the States of the Northwest, whose commerce passes over the lakes, might find their ancient right of navigation interrupted by impassable shoals, if not in the St. Clair and Detroit rivers, certainly in Lake St. Clair, the depth of whose navigable channels is now barely sufficient for the passage of our largest vessels. Here is one of the strongest cases to be put for asserting the doctrine of absolute sovereignty over navigable waters connecting with the ocean. It is not the case of a river, but a large inland sea, 340 miles long, and averaging 58 miles in width, and lying entirely within our own country. The United States have not yet claimed the right thus to drain its waters and destroy or impair the navigation of the St. Lawrence; but it implies no greater sovereignty on our part than that which Great Britain claims over that river, and one case has been supposed to illustrate the other, and to show that there can be no such right as that of *absolute* control over the mouth of a navigable river emptying into the ocean, as against a nation occupying the same river above.

Another argument may be adduced in favor of the claim of the United States, based upon the *joint acquisition* of the St. Lawrence by Great Britain and her American colonies, as the result of the war with France, followed by the treaty of 1763, which gave the Canadas to England. In that war, many of the colonies, now States of this Union, "well bore their part," and contributed not a little in accomplishing its results. From that time to the Revolution they enjoyed freely its navigation, and none can question their right during this period. But they claimed it then as *colonies;* and should they, by revolutionizing and erecting themselves into independent States and sovereignties, possess less right of navigation than before? Would it not be more reasonable to suppose that their transition from a state of colonial vassalage to one of national sovereignty would enlarge, if possible, or at least not diminish, and even destroy, their former right?

We are now brought to a consideration of the last, and perhaps the strongest, argument in favor of the American claim—that of *commercial necessity.* This argument has its origin in no temporary or artificial causes, which it is in our power to remove, but springs from that difference of geographical position to which, from the nature of things, nations must forever be subject. "The unerring counsels of nature" have led our people to the shores of the great lakes, and pointed them out as sources and parts of a great navigable highway to the ocean. Circumstances connected with the recent and wonderful growth of our country, and especially of that section which borders upon this highway, now point to its use, not merely as a convenience, but necessity. This argument presents us with a view of the trade and commerce which now seek access to the markets of the world through this channel, and invites us to estimate them, if possible, for the future. It pictures to us the valley of the lakes as it is, and is to be.

This valley contains a lake coast of about 5,000 miles, of which nearly three thousand belong to the United States. Lakes Ontario, Erie, Huron, Michigan and Superior, not including the straits and channels by which they are connected, form a continuous body of water 1,450 miles in length and averaging 61 miles in width. But few countries *can,* none but our own *does,* contain such a field for inland commerce. Its commercial importance is best exhibited by the wonderful development of population and wealth which have so suddenly accumulated upon its shores. History has never before recorded a more wonderful story in the settlement of the world than that which tells of the birth and growth of this Northwestern valley. The general settlement of our country has surpassed the most sanguine expectations; but that has been the work of centuries, whilst the settlement of this valley has been the work of a generation—of a day. There are those who saw the Northwest when it did not contain 5,000 inhabitants, and are now living to see it teeming with a population of five millions, or almost double our entire population when we declared our independence of Great Britain. Its commerce has been equally sudden in growth and wonderful in extent.

Who will not be startled on being told that the commerce of Michigan has become nearly equal to that of all Canada? Yet, incredible as it may seem, it is true. But Michigan is the child of one generation; and in our own day her population has risen from five to nearly five hundred thousand, whilst the population of Canada is more than three times that of this youthful State, and, having the experience of two centuries, she even now languishes as with premature decline.

The following is a comparative view of the commerce of Canada and Michigan, in respect to certain leading exports, for the year 1847:

	Canada exported.	Michigan exported.
Flour, bbls.	928,061	933,179
Wheat, bushels	925,012	601,688
Lumber, in feet	76,913,735	73,842,000
Shingles	14,744,000	26,633,000
Aggregate exports for 1847	(unknown)	$7,119,832

We have not the means for determining, in figures, the aggregate exports of Canada for the year 1847, but, from such information as we have been able to obtain, they are believed to have been much less than those of Michigan; but the imports of the former for the same year are known to have been greater than those of the latter. Furthermore, the trade of Canada has been, of late years, steadily declining, and has reached a point of great depression; whilst that of Michigan, as of all the Northwestern States, has been steadily increasing.

There are now eight States immediately connected with the navigation of the lakes whose commerce, to some extent, might, if permitted, seek an outlet to the ocean through the St. Lawrence—Vermont, New York, Pennsylvania, Ohio, Michigan, Indiana, Illinois, and Wisconsin. They were estimated to contain in 1846 a population of 8,877,456, or nearly half that of the whole Union, of which 2,928,925 depended upon the lakes for reaching a market. Much information upon this subject is contained in the very valuable report to the Secretary of War from the Topographical Bureau of December 10, 1847, which presents a view of the lake commerce up to the year 1846. We have drawn upon this source for a few important statistics, and do not doubt that they may be relied on as mainly correct, since they are based upon detailed reports from the various collection ports and districts, which exhibit the kinds and quantities of which the commerce consists. We have been also kindly furnished by Colonel Abert, of the Topographical Bureau, with some facts and figures touching the commerce of the lakes at a much later period; and, as they are believed not yet to have been published, they are presented below, in a consolidated form, in connexion with those for a former year:

Lake tonnage for 1846 was, steam	60,825
Do.....do.....do...sailing	46,011
Total for 1846	106,836

The upper lake tonnage for 1849, with that of Lake Ontario for 1848, exhibits a total tonnage of—that of Lake Champlain not included	198,295
Increase is nearly 100 per cent., being	91,459
Mariners employed on the lakes in 1846 were	6,972

The following table exhibits the total exports and imports of certain leading ports and districts:

Buffalo, (port,) 1846	$48,989,116
Cleveland....do	12,559,110
Detroit......do	8,706,348
Oswego......do	9,502,980
Erie........do	6,373,246
Whitehall....do	6,327,489
Monroe, (district,) and Toledo, 1846	9,519,067
Sandusky, (district,) 1846..	5,943,127
Burlington......do	3,777,726
Chicago, (port,) 1848	11,903,000
Milwaukie....do	5,927,000

The aggregate exports and imports of the lake ports for 1846 were reported at $123,829,821.

This sum, however, represents a duplicate commerce, since the exports of one place are to some extent the imports of another, and the nett value was estimated to be one-half, or $61,914,910.

This view, for 1846, falls much short of the whole truth, since it is known that these estimates include nothing for the commerce of eighteen important places, from which there were no returns for that year.

If we now look at the lake commerce for the year 1848, we find that its increase is nearly commensurate with that of the tonnage, as above stated. The aggregate exports and imports for that year of the different lakes were estimated as follows, in round numbers:

Lake Michigan, exports and imports, 1848	$24,320,000
Lake Huron......do......do....do	848,000
Lake St. Clair....do......do....do	636,000
Lake Erie.........do......do....do	115,785,000
Lake Superior.....do......do....do	(unknown.)
Total for 1848, in round numbers	141,589,000
Lake Ontario, for 1848	28,141,000
Lake Champlain..do	(unknown.)
	169,730,000

Consolidated returns in exact numbers:

Lakes above the falls	$141,593,567
Lake Ontario	28,140,927
Lake Champlain, (1846)	11,266,059
Lake Superior	(unknown.)
	181,000,553

This estimate gives the sum of $181,000,553 as the aggregate value of the lake exports and imports for the year 1848, of which, upon the principle before mentioned, one-half may be set down as the nett value for that year—$90,500,276.

Such are some few of the many facts from which some estimate may be formed of the immense commerce of the lakes. The great increase of the articles of flour and wheat, as received for a series of years prior to 1848, at Buffalo, the principal receiving depot of the lake commerce, on its way to the eastern markets, furnishes something like an index of its general increase in other productions. Reduced to an equivalent in wheat, they rose from 2,780,000 bushels in 1841 to 10,688,564 bushels in 1847; and, adopting 17 per cent. as an approved rate of annual increase of the aggregate lake commerce, in ten years, or in 1857, its nett value will be $170,545,257.

The above facts and figures enable us to form some idea of the present commercial condition of the lake valley. But who can measure its prospects in the future? The experience of the few past years teaches that its growth has surpassed all prior calculations, and past estimates have seldom kept pace with existing realities. It has become quite impossible to proportion, in advance, the increase of this region in population, wealth, and commerce, to the increase of its facilities for communicating with the eastern markets. The future refuses to be governed by rules of past experience. If the commerce of this valley is to increase from sixty-three millions in 1847 to ONE HUNDRED AND SEVENTY MILLIONS in 1857, who will undertake to measure it at the expiration of another quarter or half of a century? And if it now crowds our channels of communication almost to stoppage, and, consequently, finds its way disadvantageously through them to market, what will be the condition of things in fifty, twenty-five, or even ten years hence, unless some portion of it can find its way to the ocean through the channel of the St. Lawrence, which nature has constructed for it with so liberal a hand?

Further, we cannot overlook the very important fact that the free navigation of the St. Lawrence would, in effect, for commercial purposes, add three thousand miles to our ocean-coast. It would convert the lakes into great ocean-inlets or bays, and their ports into ocean-harbors. Whitehall, Burlington, Oswego, Buffalo, Cleveland, Detroit, Milwaukie, Chicago, and all our lake towns and cities, would be substantially upon the ocean. They could thus carry on a direct export and import trade with Liverpool, with China, or any other remote country of the globe which may be accessible from the ocean. It would open their valuable timber forests, and enable them to send ships, as well as cargoes, for sale to the English marts, or those of any other country by whose navigation laws it might be permitted. Such a change in geographical position could hardly fail to produce a great revolution in the commerce of the Northwest, not by way of diverting it seriously from its accustomed channels, but by opening new fields of enterprise, stimulating new industry, and giving new employment to labor. No apprehension need be entertained that existing artificial channels would not continue to be taxed for transportation, as now, to the extent of their capacity for public use and advantage. We have already shown the probable future increase of our lake commerce; and all apprehension like that suggested should be dispelled, when it is also considered that the population of the Northwest alone, estimating by approved principles of increase as applicable to that particular and growing region, will, in the lapse of half a century, be not far from thirty millions, or several millions greater than the present population of the entire Union.

There are also some other facts which must be noticed for the purpose of showing that the free navigation of the St. Lawrence would be revolutionary in some of its results, not by interfering with present commercial interests, but by stimulating new industry and calling for new labor. We had in 1847, as before seen, a lake tonnage of nearly 200,000 tons; and this, with its subsequent increase, is employed in short voyages, varying in time from one to a few days. But open the St. Lawrence, and these voyages may, instead of days or weeks, require months and even years. One single ocean voyage may become equal to all the voyages of a vessel which plies during every week of the navigable season between Buffalo and Chicago. For every vessel engaged in present commerce that passes out upon the ocean, another must sooner or later take its place.

All this would require more tonnage and more hands. Can it be doubted that, under the stimulus of this measure, our lake tonnage would be suddenly and vastly increased, and even quadrupled, at an early day? In this estimate we do not include the vessels which would be constructed for sale in a foreign market. Such an increase of tonnage would bring with it an increase of hands, and raise the amount of the latter from seven to twenty-eight thousand. These results would tend to produce competition, whilst competition would tend to cheapen the transportation of our commerce. To this must be added the advantages of a continuous voyage—one which would be subject to little or no delays at intermediate ports, and to no expenses for transhipment. A large portion of the expense of transportation is incurred at the places of shipment and discharge, and hence the cost of the voyage is not determined by its length. All the ports upon the lakes below Lake Superior are said to be nearer Liverpool than Odessa, the principal wheat mart on the Black sea. Cleveland is said to be more than a thousand miles nearer; so that there is little room for doubt that the lake valley, having the advantages of a continuous voyage *via* the St. Lawrence, can send its wheat as cheaply to the English markets as the country of the Black sea, and thus maintain a successful competition.

We should fail to do justice to the subject if we omitted to notice another feature in the commercial condition of the lake valley: that for at least five months in every year its navigable waters are bound up with frosts and snows of a northern winter. In 1846, the capital invested in the lake tonnage was estimated at six, and now cannot be far from ten millions; but during the long period of winter this vast capital is idle, whilst the ships are decaying at their moorings, amidst snow and ice. For this loss, it is well known, the public is obliged to pay, by a necessary and consequent increase of prices charged for the transportation of persons and property. From this cause alone are the people of the lake valley every year taxed hundreds of thousands of dollars; but it is a tax which, to some extent at least, the free navigation of the St. Lawrence would remove. Winter upon the lakes now suddenly turns thousands out of employ for nearly half a year; and, being generally unfitted, by the habits of a seafaring life, to engage in ordinary occupations upon land, to many of them but little is left save to congregate in the cities, and there viciously squander their earnings of the summer. Make free the St. Lawrence, and many of our ships, with their crews, engaged during the summer in inland commerce, at least such as are fitted for ocean navigation, would flee from the icy lakes during winter, and seek other and more genial fields of commercial enterprise.

We have now presented a brief sketch of the principal arguments upon which our claim to a free navigation of the St. Lawrence is based. It must, however, be remembered, that this exhibition of the commerce of the lakes has been confined entirely to that which is American in its character. There is also upon the lakes a large British commerce, which would be greatly increased by that reciprocal stimulus of trade which would spring from a joint and equal navigation of the river by the people of both countries.

But little, therefore, now remains, save to inquire what objections, if any, can be urged against the justice of the American claim? That it would benefit us, there is no doubt; and that it would work no injury to British commercial interests, seems equally clear. So far from that is the truth, that it would operate as a fresh stimulus of British enterprise in Canada. By what principle, then, of natural right and justice, or of international law, can England withhold from us a right of so much national importance, and one the concession of which could work no injury to her own right of navigation, or involve any sacrifice of her honor? Where a right claimed by one nation against another is an *innocent* right, and its enjoyment is essential for the public interests of the nation claiming, it is believed that the law of nations has amply provided for its recognition. "Property cannot deprive nations of the general right of travelling over the earth, in order to have a communication with each other, *for carrying on trade,* and other just reasons. The master of a country may only refuse the passage on particular occasions, where he finds it is prejudicial or dangerous." (Vattel, book 2, ch. 10, sec. 132.) The same author (in ch. 10 of same book, sec. 134) says: "A passage ought also to be granted for *merchandise;* and as this may in common be done without inconvenience, to refuse it without just reason is injuring a nation, and endeavoring to deprive it of the means of *carrying on a trade with other states;* if the passage occasion any inconvenience, any expense for the preservation of canals and highways, it may be recompensed by the rights of toll." The navigation of the St. Lawrence can be connected with that of the upper lakes only by a canal. None exists at present for that purpose within our own country; and, having no right, we of course cannot ask the privilege of transporting our commerce through the canals of Canada without rendering a just compensation.

The right of passage, where it may be innocently exercised, may be well illustrated by the case of navigable straits connecting seas, the navigation of which is common to several nations. As the rivers St. Mary, St. Clair, and Detroit have often been called straits, forming a continuous communication between some of the great lakes, so the St. Lawrence, which is but another though longer link in the chain, may be likened unto a strait. It connects the ocean, which is free to all nations, with an inland sea, whose navigation is common to the two nations which occupy its shores. And of such a case the same writer upon international law says: "He who possesses the strait cannot refuse others a passage through it, provided that passage be innocent and attended with no danger to the

State." This right of passage has been well called by Grotius, "a right interwoven with the very frame of human society;" and, if more need be added to confirm the argument, let his declaration be cited, that "a free passage through countries, *rivers*, or over any part of the sea, which belong to some particular people, ought to be allowed to those who require it for the necessary occasions of life, whether those occasions be in quest of settlements, after being driven from their own country, *or to trade with a remote nation.*"—Book 2, ch. 2, sec. 13.

Further, can any objection be drawn from the practice and opinions of the world, as exhibited in its international treaties? Here it is to be remarked, that the concession of *new* rights must not be confounded with the recognition of *old* ones. Treaties sometimes create rights, and sometimes merely acknowledge those already existing, which, though questioned to some extent, are, upon examination, found to have a just existence in nature, and independently of treaties. They are, therefore, formally asserted by one party, and acknowledged by the other, so as effectually to remove all grounds for future question or difference. Thus the thirteenth article of the treaty of Utrecht, (1713,) by which France ceded to England Newfoundland, continued to the subjects of France the use of certain fisheries upon the coasts of that island. This same right to the fisheries was recognised as belonging to France by the fifth article of the treaty of Paris, (1763,) which renewed and confirmed so much of the 13th article of the treaty of Utrecht as relates to this subject. At the treaty of Versailles (1783) these fisheries were again the subject of negotiation, and Great Britain and France readjusted the terms upon which they should be enjoyed by the respective parties. The French right of fishery was again the subject of adjustment between the parties at the treaty of Paris in 1814. From this series of negotiations it may well be argued, that the treaty of Utrecht did not create the right of fishery for France, but recognised it as one already existing, and the subsequent treaty stipulations upon the subject concerned chiefly the principles and limitations by which it should be exercised.

The third article of our treaty of 1783 with England may also be cited as in point, as it stipulated for the *continued* right on our part to enjoy the fisheries in the Gulf of St. Lawrence and on the coast and banks of Newfoundland, "and at all other places in the sea, where the inhabitants of both countries used at any time heretofore to fish." Was it not obviously the intention of the parties to this stipulation not to *create*, but to *acknowledge*, for and as against each other, rights already existing, and which had existed and been enjoyed in common at least since the acquisition of Canada? These rights to the fisheries were thus admitted to belong to the United States, notwithstanding their separation from the mother country. The language of the article is, "that the people of the United States shall *continue* to enjoy" the fisheries, and thus *continues* without *creating* a right. This continuance was evidently based not upon an idea of concession on the part of England, but upon principles of natural justice and right, having their origin in the fact, that it was partly American enterprise that had discovered, explored, and occupied these fisheries.

The United States contended for such principles as these in settling the terms of the convention of 1818. England sought to maintain that the war of 1812 had abrogated the American right to the fisheries, whilst Mr. Rush, who conducted the negotiations on our part, insisted upon that right as being permanent or perpetual in its nature, as old at least as the treaty of 1783; and he shaped the terms of the convention upon this subject, with an express design on his part of excluding "the implication of the fisheries secured to us being a new grant."

The case is conceived to be analogous, and it would be difficult to show, that the natural right of the United States to transport their commerce upon the St. Lawrence to and from the ocean is much less than that, which they enjoy to the northeastern fisheries.

The question of the free navigation of the Mississippi also well illustrates the view now submitted. At the treaty of 1783 with Great Britain, its mouth was held by Spain. It formed our western boundary, and its sources were supposed to lie within British territory. Each party stipulated in this treaty for the free and joint navigation of the river. But did either party *concede* to or *create* in the other any supposed new right? Did this stipulation amount to anything more than a recognition or declaration of right as against each other, and a claim or assumption of it as against Spain? It was in fact an acknowledgment of supposed pre-existing right—a right freely to use and navigate the river, as a great highway to the ocean, which nature had created for the accommodation of the nations who might dwell upon its banks. The sources of the river were, however, subsequently ascertained to be entirely within our own boundaries, and we were left alone to assert our right against Spain. Our representatives at Madrid were instructed to press upon her attention not the privilege merely, but the *right* of freely navigating the Mississippi to its mouth; and so anxious were the American people upon this subject, and so well satisfied of the right, that the question threatened at some future time to involve us in a war with that country; but the far-seeing policy of Mr. Jefferson, which looked to the acquisition of Louisiana, settled it by the treaty of cession in 1803. It may, then, well be asked, can England now justly deny to us a principle, in reference to the mouth of the St. Lawrence, which she has already asserted against Spain, in reference to that of the Mississippi?

Nor, it is believed, can any objection to the American claim, as being against the practice or law of nations, be derived from treaties amongst the nations of Europe, which relate to the use of navigable rivers. They are believed to have proceeded in part upon the idea not of creating, but of affirming rights; not of conceding privileges, but of recognising rights which had a prior existence under the natural law. There are in Europe many rivers which are not by nature navigable, but are made so by clearing out their channels and by other artificial means, such as the Elbe, Maese, Weser, and Oder. In such cases, both reason and international law justify the exaction of tolls, to meet the expense of putting and keeping them in navigable condition; but this exaction should be limited to such special and necessary purposes.

By the treaty of Paris (1814) between England and France, the navigation of the Rhine, from the point where it becomes navigable unto the sea, was declared to be free. At this time a congress of European nations had already been proposed, and, in anticipation of its sitting, this same treaty provided, that such congress should "examine and determine in what manner the above provisions can be extended to other rivers which, in their navigable course, separate or traverse different States."

The congress of Vienna seems manifestly to have proceeded upon the principle of recognising the right of nations freely to navigate to its mouth the same river, which separates or crosses their territories as a pre-existing right, founded in nature and confirmed in national convenience and necessity. By the general treaty, (June 9, 1815,) all those "powers, whose States are separated or crossed by the same navigable river," stipulated that their navigation, "along their whole course, from the point where each of them becomes navigable to its mouth, shall be entirely free, and shall not, *in respect to commerce,* be prohibited to any one." (See arts. 108 and 109, Herzlet's Commercial Treaties, vol. 1.) Article 96 of the same treaty provided specially that its principles concerning the navigation of rivers should be applicable to the Po. To this treaty were appended certain articles intended to operate as a uniform system of police for *regulating* their navigation; also, a set of articles providing specially for the free navigation of the Rhine, and another set providing for that of the Neckar, Mayne, Moselle, Meuse, and Scheldt, from the point where each of them becomes navigable to their mouths."

We have thus the voice of nearly all Europe sanctioning the principle contended for; for nearly all Europe was party to this treaty. In respect to the navigation of rivers, the treaty acts in part upon rights already supposed to exist. It asserts and *regulates,* without *creating* them. As the statute often merely affirms the common law, so this treaty affirms the international and natural law; and the action of the Vienna congress upon this subject had its origin not so much in a denial of the right of nations to freely navigate rivers which separate or cross their territories, as in the necessity of agreeing upon some uniform regulations for using it, and freeing it from those embarrassments which might otherwise flow from the various and conflicting regulations of different States. Whatever may have been the ancient doctrine respecting national sovereignty over the mouths of navigable rivers emptying into the ocean, the British claim to an absolute control over the mouth of the St. Lawrence should now be considered as inconsistent with a liberal and enlightened application of the natural law, and with the principles recognised by the general treaty of Vienna, to which England was a prominent party.

If the American Union had never been formed, or if each of its States were now to become suddenly invested with full national sovereignty, a case would exist very analogous to that, which made the navigable rivers of Europe an important and even necessary subject for adjustment by the congress of Vienna. In either of such events, what State would presume to assert against another absolute control over the waters of a navigable river, which should separate or traverse the territories of both? Who shall close the mouth of the Connecticut? Who shut up the Delaware, and drive the ships of Philadelphia from its waters? What single State shall barricade the Mississippi against the commerce of St. Louis, Cincinnati, and all the great States and Territories situate upon its banks, or those of its vast tributaries, which stretch from the Alleghanies to the Rocky mountains?

To these questions there can be but one answer—"None." The eternal principles of justice—the laws of nature—answer, "None." But, in either of the supposed cases, our navigable rivers would become the theatres of various contending interests, and necessarily subject to a variety of local jurisdictions. To avoid all differences and conflicts which might naturally flow from such variety of interest and jurisdiction, a congress of

States, like that of Vienna, might well assemble for the purpose of affirming, by treaty, for and against each other, the right of freely navigating those rivers by which they might be separated or crossed, and of regulating its exercise by principles of fairness and uniformity. The case has been supposed for illustration; and is it not evident, that such a treaty would not *create* the right of navigation, but simply *affirm* and *recognise* it as one pre-existing? Such a treaty would declare an existing right, and provide for its equal and peaceful enjoyment.

We have thus far considered the free navigation of the St. Lawrence as the subject of a claim on the part of our government under the law of nature and of nations. We have done this, that the question may be viewed in its whole extent, and that, should the views and arguments submitted in favor of the American claim as one of right not be regarded as *conclusive*, they may at least appear as reasons, why the British government should now generously concede to us a privilege, in support of which so much can be urged, and to which time has added value and importance. If it cannot be secured as a right, then it is to be considered as a privilege, to be acquired either by treaty or by some reciprocal legislation, based upon the idea of rendering a just equivalent.

If England will not acknowledge the right, as conferred upon us by the hand of nature, she should acknowledge it by treaty. She should, accordin to her view, *create* it, and confer it upon us with her own hand. She should do it, too, with the generosity of nature, without money and without price. She should do it with a magnanimity which so well becomes her position. To her it can work no injury, whilst to us it is a measure of great advantage. Why should she not grant to us, in respect to the mouth of the St. Lawrence, what she asserted against Spain in 1783, in respect to that of the Mississippi? Why not yield to us what, in 1814, she demanded from France in relation to the Rhine? Why not follow now her own enlightened example at Vienna, when she demanded of Europe the free navigation of the Po, the Scheldt, and other rivers, which did not wash a foot of British soil?

But, if England will neither acknowledge the right as already existing, nor confer it upon us as a gratuity, then it can only be acquired by purchase, on the rendition of some just equivalent. We have already, under another view of the subject, presented those considerations which now conspire to render the free navigation of the St. Lawrence a question of present and practical importance. If the *right* be denied, they yet weigh in favor of acquiring the *privilege*, and it is unnecessary to repeat them. If it is to be purchased by treaty, then it presses itself upon the attention of the treaty-making power, as a question which, if not soon settled by negotiation, must ere long be settled by the irresistible course of human events. But if it is to be purchased by means of reciprocal legislation, then it urges itself upon the attention of Congress, and calls for the adoption of legislative measures with a view to its acquisition. Whatever difference of opinion may exist as to the mode by which it should be acquired, it seems very certain, that the question in regard to the St. Lawrence, which so earnestly engaged the attention of the administrations of Monroe and the younger Adams, and which Mr. Adams and Mr. Clay, as they successively stood at the head of the State Department, pressed upon the attention of the British government with so much ability and patriotism, is now revived with increased magnitude. Nor is the fact to be disguised, that the sudden growth of the lake valley, its increased and increasing commerce, its convenience, its wants, its dearest interests, the petitions of its people, and circumstances connected with the geographical relations of the two countries, and their future peace and harmony, are all conspiring to present the question as one, whose early settlement is suggested by the soundest dictates of justice, prudence, and wisdom.

ALEX. W. BUEL.
JOHN A. McCLERNAND.*
E. G. SPAULDING.

[* Mr. McClernand signs the foregoing report, meaning thereby to affirm the following principles, which are understood by him to be substantially affirmed by the report, viz :

1st. That by natural law, the right of navigating a stream or river is the equal and common right of all the inhabitants upon its borders. 2d. That by the law of society, upon the establishment of a local jurisdiction over a part of the river, the pre-existing natural right of navigating that part becomes subject to modification by the local sovereign. 3d. That the right thus remaining still holds good for the purpose of innocent exercise or use, and is denominated an imperfect right; but is, nevertheless, an essential and real right. 4th. That the obstruction or refusal of this right, when not called for by the peace or safety of the local sovereign, and to the injury of the inhabitants above, is a wrong, which may authorize demand for redress .]

www.ingramcontent.com/pod-product-compliance
Lightning Source LLC
LaVergne TN
LVHW011145110826
845150LV00008B/2529
9781418192204